Keepsakes for
the Journey

Series Preface

The volumes in NCP's "7 x 4" series offer a meditation a day for four weeks, a bite of food for thought, a reflection that lets a reader ponder the spiritual significance of each and every day. Small enough to slip into a purse or coat pocket, these books fit easily into everyday routines.

Keepsakes for the Journey

Four Weeks on
Faith Deepening

Susan Muto

New City Press
Hyde Park, New York

I dedicate this book to my colleague, co-author, and soul-friend, Father Adrian van Kaam, C.S.Sp., Ph.D. (1920–2007), who once said, "There are no coincidences, only providences." Our life in service of others has validated the truth of this keepsake.

Published in the United States by New City Press
202 Comforter Blvd., Hyde Park, NY 12538
www.newcitypress.com
©2010 Susan Muto

Cover design by Durva Correia

Library of Congress Cataloging-in-Publication Data:

Muto, Susan Annette.
  Keepsakes for the journey : four weeks on faith deepening / Susan Muto.
      p. cm. — (A meditation a day for a span of four weeks)
  Includes bibliographical references.
  ISBN 978-1-56548-333-0 (pbk. : alk. paper) 1. Meditations. I. Title.
  BV4832.3.M89 2010
  248.4'82—dc22
                                    2009043040

Printed in the United States of America

Contents

Foreword 7

one
Rejoice Always

1. Vision of the Beyond 10
2. Love's Eternal Flame 12
3. Searching for Words 14
4. Sent by God to Serve 16
5. Healing Power of Simplicity 18
6. Moved by Love 20
7. Mystery at Our Feet 22

two
Pray Without Ceasing

1. Gift of Contemplation 26
2. Conversations with God 28
3. Connecting Contemplation and Action 30
4. Wellsprings of Prayer 32
5. Release through Repentance 34
6. Christ at the Center 36
7. God Known and Unknown 38

three
Give Thanks in All Circumstances

1. Singing in Silence 42
2. Be on Guard 44
3. Receiving Christ in Our Soul 46
4. Caring for One Another 48
5. Willing Each Other to Be 50
6. Freedom of Soul 52
7. To Lose Is to Gain 54

four
Do Not Quench the Spirit

1. Listening to Our Heart 58
2. Mending Our Ways 60
3. Love Flowing Between Us 62
4. From Trials to Triumphs 64
5. Unflinching Faith 66
6. Following the Spirit's Leading 68
7. True Worship 70

Bibliography 72

Foreword

In a throw-away culture like our own, keepsakes and other collectibles become more a necessity than a luxury. A cracked cup from which we drank hot chocolate as a child. A ragged teddy bear we refuse to discard. A dog-eared postcard from our favorite hide-a-way. A faded pearl necklace or a tie worn once too often but worth keeping as a memory of being with that special someone.

Keepsakes that focus on life's purpose and our personal mission prevent us from feeling like empty shells tossed hither and yon on the shores of this all too brief existence. It demoralizes us to have no sense of where the day has gone. Short or long as our life may be, we need to treat each moment on earth as if it were our last.

The things with which we do not want to part may have little or no monetary value. We treasure them not as possessions but as memory banks to retain when life loses its meaning and we feel as unstable as twigs tossing wildly on a stormy sea. These precious keepsakes remind us that life may look chaotic but there is a plan to it.

Keepsakes influence the way we view the connection between what we do and who we are. Rather than serving only the expansion of our own ego, they invite us to link our life to a higher purpose freed from any fixation on self-adulation. Each of us has known on some level the longing to be a free spirit whose self-sacrificing ways are worthy of emulation. Without in the least forfeiting the uniqueness of our call, we do what we can to advance the common good. A life like this, full of meaning, makes every keepsake an epiphany of sorts. It proves to us, despite onslaughts of doubt, that there is a hopeful thread binding our lives together. To touch these treasures is to come to the conclusion that we are not masters of our fate but servants of a mystery we may glimpse in time but never fathom totally.

Many years ago a friend gave me a "birthday book" from the Metropolitan Museum of Art in New York City. It commemorates, with lovely reproductions of their masterworks, the birthdays of celebrated painters, sculptors, architects, print makers, photographers, and other creative geniuses. On the blank spaces under the dates of the year, I began to collect brief sayings by classical and contemporary spiritual writers whose words are keepsakes by anyone's standards. As Saint Augustine of Hippo once said, "Feed your soul in divine readings; they will prepare for you a spiritual feast."

I found in texts taken from a variety of sources, a banquet table for heart and mind whose meaning transcended every time bound era. Recording these gems and then reflecting upon them helped me to discern the hidden insights they contained. Our mission may be subtle or overt, appreciated or taken for granted, but it plays a role in the providential plan of God. Every detail of our ordinary existence has the potential to radiate a quality of presence, a depth of participation, that coincide with true discipleship. My hope is that this book will be an oasis in your busy day. May these already treasured words resonate in your soul, nourish your spirit, and inspire you to love and serve others now and for all ages to come.

Rejoice Always

one

Vision of the Beyond

> ... A child's quite touching epiphany, seeing prayer
> and the search for God not as a fleeting vision,
> isolated from the events of this world,
> but as a means of connecting oneself
> to the ordinary moments of living.
>
> —*Robert Coles*

A touching epiphany from our own childhood — laughing with glee in a little backyard pool; flying a kite for the first time and longing for it to soar out of sight; hiding from everyone calling our name in a secret corner of the garden; inviting disbelieving adults to listen to the grass grow — may never be forgotten. In the innocence of these pristine years, we seem to have no problem standing with ease on the cutting edge between time and eternity. One event flows into the other — a family drive to church, a favorite meal, a springtime planting, a wintery day, a downhill race on a flying saucer sled.

Robert Coles is correct in suggesting that the gift of childhood we must need to restore is that of "making connections" between these unforgettable events and the ordinary moments of daily living. Of equal importance is restoration of the bond we felt between ourselves and other people, including our capacity to befriend whoever crossed our path. Trust is a risk children take before they learn to distrust a stranger.

Prayer comes as naturally to their lips as play to their limbs. Whatever our age we must not lose touch with the peace and harmony praying with the heart of a child grants to us.

The docility of childlike trust gives rise to the inner ability to make ourselves available to any word the Spirit may use to awaken us to "what no eye has seen, nor ear heard [of] what God has prepared for those who love him" (1 Cor 2:9). Docility quiets our mind and opens our heart to expected and unexpected manifestations of the presence of God.

This gentling of mind and heart unblocks the obstacles that prevent us from being faithful to God's will. Docility cuts through the imprisoning bars of anxious preoccupation with "the events of this world." It lets us savor the lasting freedom of the children of God that is our spiritual legacy.

Prayer: *Lord, you embraced with laughter the children who leapt into your lap. You told those jaded by life, hard-edged and disillusioned, impatient and unfree, that unless they became like one of these, the doors to your earthly and heavenly reign would be closed to them. Help us to see in childlike faith the thread that ties together all strands of your creation. Let the power of your Spirit connect us to these ordinary moments so that we may catch a glimpse of their extraordinary splendor.*

2 Love's Eternal Flame

> Now each expression that we make of love
> makes life anew, our lives a single life,
> the two made one.
> In tenderness and play we lift the dark,
> and in this joyous game we keep alight
> our candle's living flame.
>
> —*Madeleine L'Engle*

The highest hurdles seem like the lowest hills when heart reaches out to heart and two people become one in spirit. Hate divides. It needs the soil of injustice in which to thrive. Love unites. It gives us all the room we need to exercise patience and to enjoy play. The healing power of love spreads into every corner of a cold heart. Love, as L'Engle says, is a joyous game in which everyone wins. Out of the blue, a friend phones, a co-worker gives us a genuine compliment, a friendly smile, an approving nod.

Any confirmation of our dignity lights up the shadows of an otherwise bleak day. As Martin Luther King, Jr. once said: "I've decided to stick with love; hate's too heavy a burden to bear." Transformation through love mirrors the butterfly effect. A once stubborn student, who refused to be taught, may be lucky enough to be loved by a dedicated teacher. Soon he sheds his thick skin like a cocoon encasing a caterpillar and becomes a star pupil.

Despite the shadow of sin that veils our earthly existence, Christ's love draws us into this "joyous game." He reminds us who hunger and thirst to "keep alight our candle's living flame" that our hope is not in vain. Redeemed by his healing love is the sadness that dampens our joy. Restored is our sense of the "tenderness and play" characteristic of this pristine state of original delight. Although our first innocence is far from us, Christ opens the door to our second innocence. He gives us a chance to reclaim the gifts of childlike wonder and undiluted trust. We are, as scripture proclaims, our brothers' and our sisters' keepers whose love for one another "makes life anew."

Prayer: *Lord, you loved us to the point of death, yet we allow vices like avarice and lust to deflate our duty to care for one another. Our need for pleasure makes us oblivious to another's pain. Being possessed by our possessions closes our ears to the cry of the poor. Nothing can snap open the shackles of egocentric indifference swifter than the liberating touch of other-centered love. One of the chief lessons you taught us, Lord, was to counter the acid rain of rancor with the softening waters of forgiveness. When our candle of care burns low, rekindle the flame. Draw us again into this joyous dance of love and its continuous rhythms of cordiality and compassion.*

3 Searching for Words

> Human speech is like a cracked kettle
> on which we tape crude rhythms
> for bears to dance to while we long
> to make music that will melt the stars.
>
> —Gustav Flaubert

Beautiful, grammatically correct, courteous, and compassionate words have all too often been crushed like sand under the lashing waves of curses spat out in rage. Tongues curled with expressions too scurrilous to repeat, like buckshot, crack open every target in sight!

When speech has been reduced to crude rhythms, hardly fit for bears to dance to, we demean whatever it means to be human. We choose insults over inspirations, crudeness over kindness, blasphemy over blessings. We become in a way like animals ourselves — grunting, panting, and preying on one another. We live in ignorance of the true transcendent thrust of our spirit. Yet all is not lost as long as the desire "to make music that will melt the stars" haunts our soul.

Words spoken with utter honesty consume deceptions like fire devouring an overgrown forest. Politically manipulated but implausible promises may deceive those hungry for power, but they fail to sway the thoughtful, who long to hear words worth remembering for ages hence. When speech attains the integrity of a classical composition, like Abraham Lincoln's *Gettysburg Address*, it has the power to change a nation.

The messages of Martin Luther King, Jr. were so uplifting that not even death could stifle their proclamation of respect for human dignity. The often slurred utterances of an aging Pope John Paul II were so inspiring they drew cheers and tears from his listeners. Both of these imitators of Jesus Christ practiced total lingual integrity. Their words remind us that we deserve more than drumbeats suitable for dancing bears. When we have been given the capacity to melt the hardest of hearts, why would we settle for the bad fruits of lingual depletion?

Prayer: *Lord, you spoke words weighted with truth that do not pass away. Your words stand fast in the face of evil's defiance of your law. May our response to forces beyond our control transform a sense of fatalistic surrender into a faithful yielding to the music of eternity. Give us the courage to cancel from our vocabulary words used to hurt, not heal; to curse, not console; to batter, not bless. Draw us into those wellsprings of silence out of which words of truth pour forth. Protect us from people who use words as weapons of abuse, as propaganda to subdue free spirits, as tricks of mental and spiritual entrapment. Soften the remnants of hardness in our heart that we may hear and heed your word until that day when all words fall silent and we enter into the wordless radiance of your risen presence.*

4 Sent by God to Serve

> Whatever the trials of the moment,
> whatever the hardships or sufferings,
> more important than all of these
> was the knowledge that they had been
> sent by God and served his divine providence.
>
> —*Father Walter J. Ciszek, S.J.*

In the face of such horrors as the death of the innocent in war and famine, the inhumanity of concentration camps, the relentless oppression of the poor, the greed of the powerful, we face a stark choice: either we allow the finger of divine providence to point to their meaning or we risk going out of our minds with grief and despair.

Hardships go hand in hand with the human condition. No one is immune from a sudden illness, a failed mission, a natural disaster. However successful we may be, suffering and infirmity are our common fate. The sheer fact of loss is less important than the knowledge we are meant to derive from it. The gift of wisdom does not seem to be lodged in the analytical part of our brain. Its source is attunement to reality and total reliance on the truth of God's word revealed in Holy Scripture. The mystery reminds us that "Even before a word is on my tongue, O Lord, you know it completely" (Ps 139:4) and that "… even the hairs of your head are counted" (Mt 10:30).

Between us and the Lord, there are no coincidences, only providences. However hard this truth is to grasp, nothing about our life is a pure accident; all events have been sent our way by God as invitations, challenges, and appeals pertinent to the plan of our salvation. Our role is to seek their significance and to believe, without the shadow of a doubt, that we have a place in this grand design of redemption and an important role to play.

This hope in "divine providence" rests not on human power but on the power of God. It lives on when there are no miracles, no consolations. It refuses to take refuge in scornful pessimism. In contrast to hopelessness, resignation, or pessimistic acceptance of a predetermined fate, hope connotes an expectation of joy. It does not rely on accurate predictions or problem-solving techniques. It is an act of supreme confidence in the word of God, who made heaven and earth. The Apostle Paul says, "Hope does not disappoint, because the love of God has been poured out into our hearts through the Holy Spirit that has been given to us" (Rm 5:5).

Prayer: *Lord, when we lose our footing on the firm ground of faith, show us once again that what happens to us serves a higher purpose and that every moment of life sheds light on our blessed beginning and our destined end. All that obscures your providence is our own inability to believe that you hold us in being. Whether we know it or not, we live in your embrace as children snuggling safe and sound in their parents' arms.*

5 Healing Power of Simplicity

> God has called upon us to enlighten consciences,
> not to confuse or coerce them.
> God asks us to speak with simplicity,
> not to complicate matters or to flatter
> the tastes of an audience.
> God has called upon us to heal our brothers
> [and sisters], not to frighten them.
>
> —*Pope John XXIII*

Pope John's kindly voice of compassion comes through the text of this encouraging message. It seems as if his aim is to relieve symptoms of false guilt, to calm our fears, to convince us that God's gentle hand touches hurt souls in need of healing. The Pope challenges us not to forget our shared calling in Christ. Our role in his Mystical Body is to enlighten consciences by word and deed, by contemplative prayer and charitable work. Our place is not to coerce others to profess shallow acts of faith but to wait with them for the grace of ongoing conversion.

In a world of double talk, where lying becomes the favorite ploy of politicians and ordinary citizens, the Pope points to the opposite way our Divine Teacher addresses us. He brings clarity out of confusion. He comes to show us the path to simplicity.

By contrast, falsehood of any sort makes our lives incredibly complex. Marital infidelity offers perhaps the most convincing example of what happens when one follows this crooked maze. One lie leads to another. Intricate schemes of deception tear open the delicate fabric of trust and forgiveness.

Our role as disciples of Christ is not to complicate matters already tied in knots by our fallen condition. We must try to put into practice the plain and simple truths our Master teaches. To maintain a prophetic voice, we must have the courage to be counter-cultural. Following Christ is not a smart way to win popularity contests by flattering others to gain their approval. We have to be prepared to rub people the wrong way when we choose to do what is right.

The Pope displays the tender concern of a loving father by reminding us that we are here to forgive others, not to frighten them; to heal broken hearts, not to harm them by deceit. It is not our place to depict to poor sinners the punishment that awaits them but to show them the face of the Good Shepherd on whose care they can rely.

Prayer: *Lord, thank you for engaging the likes of us to enlighten others about the gratuity of your grace. Grant us the clarity of mind and courage of spirit we need to abide in your word and proclaim your truth. How easy it would be to lose ourselves in a tangled web of lies. Without your teaching to guide us, we would be like a herd of lost sheep, pushed from one dry field of deception to the next. You alone can heal the wounds of sin that complicate our world. Transfuse the saving power of your body and blood into our timid hearts until perfect love casts out all fear* (cf. 1 Jn 4:18).

6 Moved by Love

... It is peculiar to being to be bourne along
by an immense movement,
a movement that can only take on
concrete and living meaning for the mind
if it continues to find new motives
for loving everywhere.

—Louis Lavelle

When the strains of life remind us of our vulnerability, we need to experience the sensation of being carried by a Spirit stronger than we are. To flow with this movement is to cultivate the unconditional love we have already received.

A hint as to how we ought to behave comes to light in the notion of *continuity* expressed in acts of love that give us new motives to care for one another. Wherever we turn there are hands outstretched that need to be held. There are friends and strangers who deserve our help. Our goal before God is not to develop a savior complex but to practice the charitable outreach required of us by virtue of our being "called his disciples" (Lk 6:13).

God knows we are all wounded, broken, vulnerable people in need of redemption. Our place is neither to judge nor to condemn this suffering state but to put balm on one another's battle scars and to bathe each other's feet.

The joyful fruits of self-giving service may lead us to recall a religion teacher who could not do enough for her students; a doctor who spent quality time at the bedside of her patients; a pastor who so loved God's word that those who listened to his sermons never forgot them. These exemplary servants live on in our memory because others, not themselves, were the center of their world.

Giving of ourselves to God's children is at times a draining experience, but it can also be surprisingly energizing. We help others only to find that they are the ones who help us. This outcome may startle us until we remember that whatever we do for the least of these we do for our Lord (cf. Mt 25:45). This scriptural revelation carries us beyond the misery of an ungenerous spirit to the joyful ministry of doing the Lord's work in unnoticed ways that reveal "new motives for loving everywhere."

Prayer: *Lord, your love assures us that we never walk alone. On the perilous path of life's unpredictable changes, we know that you are at our side, carrying us in the bad times, encouraging us in the good. Enlighten the eyes of our heart that we may see in faith that you are nearer to us than we are to ourselves. Grant us day by day new reasons for living generously. Let us be and become witnesses to the care and compassion that cause others to rejoice in the love you radiate through the least of us.*

7 Mystery at Our Feet

> Life is a mystery, love is a delight.
> Therefore I take it as axiomatic that one should settle
> for nothing less than the infinite mystery
> and the infinite delight, i.e., God.
> In fact I demand it.
> I refuse to settle for anything less.
> —Walker Percy

The coward in us would slide down the slippery slope of settling for less but not the kind of Christian Walker Percy is. What do we gain if we compromise the pursuit of excellence? Are we naive enough to believe that customers do not notice when shopkeepers falsify measurements and shortchange them? Examples of injustice abound in society today. All too many of us slip out of church before the final blessing, content to live only a lukewarm faith.

This situation can change when every duty becomes a delight. Our refusal to follow the path to mediocrity is proven by the fact that we do treat others as we expect them to treat us. We neither lie nor cheat nor steal. We take nothing for granted when we practice the "thank you" prayer: "Thank you, Lord, for the cup of tea that warms me on this winter morning, for the fact that my car starts, for the friendly attendant who accepts my toll payment." Everyone we meet and everything we do is another reason to rejoice always. We refuse to settle for less when God calls us to so much more. The Divine Presence in whose light we live cancels the temptation to self-idolatry. We cease to follow our whims as if they were God's will.

Attempts to master the mystery are not uncommon. Horoscopes pretend to supply answers to life's most burning questions. How-to books cover every topic from lack of sexual satisfaction in marriages to techniques that guarantee swift access to the transcendent. Some seem to live by the myth that there is nothing we cannot control once we set our minds to it.

Walker Percy does not believe in this hype nor should we. "Life is a mystery." It defies what reason can grasp. It is not a game we can win simply by becoming clever deal-makers. Only in faith can we cope with its burdens and blessings. All we know in the end is that "love is a delight" that transcends our expectations. Adversity advances rather than retards our journey to the stars.

Prayer: *Lord, the desires for the "more than" you awaken in us cannot be crushed by even the most severe disappointments. No matter what happens, we must not settle for less. Every time we drift aimlessly on the surface of life, you beckon us to dive into the ocean depths of your love. On this razor's edge between the finite and the infinite, we have a purpose to fulfill, a destiny to reach. Teach us not to walk with heads lowered to accommodate what is less but to set our eyes on what is always more: the Alpha and the Omega, the beginning and the end.*

two

Pray Without Ceasing

Gift of Contemplation

> Contemplation is a free and clear vision
> of the mind fixed upon the manifestation
> of wisdom in suspended wonder.
>
> —Richard of Saint Victor

Contemplation unbinds us from whatever prevents us from enjoying the beautiful experience of pure adoration of God. How often our hearts ache from being torn in a thousand pieces! We look and feel distraught. What a relief it is to fix our scattered minds on one word or phrase from Holy Scripture. Every time we drift away, we return to this homeport. We are present to it in stillness. The text becomes for us a "manifestation of wisdom." In its many layers of meaning, we find food for our soul.

To be in a state of "suspended wonder" preserves the awe disposition. It prevents us from slipping into cynicism. It is as if we see with sudden clarity the unveiling of the mystery in what we once beheld as merely mundane.

To be led to these moments of wordless wonder, we need to cultivate ways to calm ourselves on every level of our being — physical, mental, emotional, and spiritual. Such quieting readies us to receive contemplative insights that change for the better the way we used to be.

Saint John of the Cross, the sixteenth-century Spanish mystic who, along with Saint Teresa of Avila, reformed the Carmelite order, says of this turning point that it marks our departure from a former way of life, sunk in selfish sensuality, to the dawning of a new life in Christ. The foolish and deceptive habits that imprisoned our spirit undergo purgation. The irony is that despite such suffering we feel more free. We accept that the armor of our willfulness must be melted in the fire of God's love so that it can be permanently reformed. In "suspended wonder" we hold fast to the truth that "… just as Christ was raised from the dead by the glory of the Father, so we too might walk in the newness of life" (Rm 6:4).

Prayer: *Lord, when shadows of doubt cloud our ability to discern the subtle movements that signify your will, clear our vision so that we may follow your lead without fear or hesitation. Let the serene waters of baptism revive our souls, calming useless worry and the distractions that destroy worship. Remove the blinders from our eyes so that we may behold your face and be healed of whatever has paralyzed our capacity to live in pure faith when the "why" of wonder remains a mystery.*

2 Conversations with God

> There is no mode of life in the world
> more pleasing and more full of delight
> than continual conversation with God.
> —*Brother Lawrence of the Resurrection*

The difference between a voice crying in the wilderness and a void empty of meaning; between a God who knows us better than we know ourselves and an indifferent watchmaker who sets the universe in motion and retires to a distant galaxy beyond our reach; between the give-and-take of good friends and a monotone muttered by us but heard by no one, is dialogue with the Divine.

Between us and God there ought to be a steady stream of pleasing chatter that gives our friendship staying power. Nothing the world has to offer can compare with the self-offering of God to us. Our Beloved does not retreat from the messiness of the world into the majesty of eternity. Emmanuel has chosen to be "God-with-us," to embrace our wounded condition and to weep in the face of our loss. He engages us in an intimacy that includes every facet of living and dying. When life is delightful, it is easy to talk about it. Not so when we hover on the edge of despair. We are loathe to converse politely with God or anyone else. We would rather rant and rave.

Brother Lawrence would reply that candid conversation with one who loves us and wills our good leaves room for anger. Real talk ceases when we repress our feelings and fail to practice the presence of God. To converse with the Divine about the details of daily life is as simple as saying, "Lord, I wish I had more to bring before you than this load of dirty laundry, but I might as well make the best of it. Be with me as I sort through these garments, fill the washing machine, adjust the proper setting …"

Fully awake and falling asleep, scouring pots and pans and finding our pew in church, driving the car and searching for a parking space — in these and myriad other instances we try to stay in touch with the Trinity. The advice given by this holy brother, simple as it is, has a lofty goal: to show us that the way to sanctity stretches along the very path on which we now trod.

Prayer: *Lord, how foolish we are to treat you as if you were a distant deity unconcerned about the details of day-to-day life. That deception is overcome by the grace of continual conversation. With a technique as simple as talk, we enjoy the privilege of walking in your company, of becoming one with that great cloud of witnesses, praising your glory. You are the beginning and the end of our story and all that happens in between. You are there to stave off our woes, to cushion our defects, and to celebrate our joys. Since you know us through and through, we can discuss everything with you.*

3. Connecting Contemplation and Action

> … What I still ask for daily — for life
> as long as I have work to do
> and work as long as I have life.
>
> —*Reynolds Price*

Sentiments such as these caution us not to focus on the drudgery of daily labor but on the joy of functioning. Work becomes ennobling when we see in what we do an expression of who we are. We dare to speak in awe of the sanctity of service, of the contemplative core of every action from planting a garden to praying for rain. Every task we do with love becomes a pointer to the nobility of labor.

Rather than being swamped by the pressures of time urgency, the challenge we face is to remain in the presence of the Lord. However distracted we are, we can discipline ourselves to return inwardly to the hermitage of our heart. In this way we avoid the split between contemplation and action. It becomes second nature to us to live from this center and to be responsive to the graces we receive. Waking or sleeping, working or in worship, engaged in ministry or pausing for moments of recollection, we seek to unite ourselves to God.

To connect *ora* (prayer) and *labora* (work) prevents any split between spirituality and functionality.

Sloth, sluggishness, procrastination, a day without one good deed to show for it, are the sins good workers are loathe to commit. Doing the trivial tasks of daily life in service of the Lord explains why we are here: to be in partnership with our Creator and so to leave behind some sign of our purpose in this world. We do not want to pass through life like a shadow. Work unites us to the Divine Worker. It is the window through which we strive to help ourselves and others in just, peaceful, and merciful ways.

This practice is never an excuse to escape from reality into a dream world of mystical consolations. The opposite is true. It puts us in touch with whatever cross God asks us to carry as well as with whatever causes us to rejoice. Being in God's presence is the secret to doing everything well, to sacrificing time and energy for Christ's sake. In sorrow and in joy, in loss and in gain, we remain in God's presence. It is the air we breathe in time as a forecast of eternity.

Prayer: *Lord, we who are the work of your hands, thank you for giving us hands with which to work. When we fold them in prayer, we remember our partnership with you, the source and center of our lives. The smallest act of love sends waves of gratitude through every member of your Mystical Body. May the labor we do on earth mirror in some way what you do without ceasing for our benefit. With the gifts we have been given, let your will be done on earth as it is in heaven.*

4 Wellsprings of Prayer

> Silence ... is the mother of prayer.
> It frees the prisoner; it guards the divine flame;
> it watches over reasoning;
> it protects the sense of penitence.
>
> —John Climacus

If we cannot find silence in a world plugged into headphones, we must look for it in our hearts. Rare as such moments may be, we cannot live humane lives without them. The noise pulsating within us interferes with our listening to the timid whispers of the Holy Spirit. The higher its volume, the more it inclines us to run away from these God-guided inspirations.

All of us in some way are in bondage to the pulsation of speed, causing us to make careless decisions and to feel as if fast-lane living eats our days away. Yet silence, like a fierce warrior of faith, teaches us to banish our fears, to let go of our disappointments, and to quiet the endless litany of "why's" and "what for's" that beat upon our tired brain.

Silence allows the mind and the heart to act in unison. It reveals the sly deceptions attributed to the reasoning process and challenges us to confess them in compunction. It frees us to face the truth of who we are, which no amount of noise can stifle.

Silence lets us pause, at least for a brief duration, to regain our perspective. This stepping aside in silence could be compared to looking at a painting. From afar, we enjoy its beauty and wholeness; we appreciate the depth of the artist's sensitivity. However, if we stand too close to the canvas, we may miss the beauty of the work as a whole and see only the chips and cracks on the surface. Lacking this hush of quiet appreciation, we may miss the full harmony the painting reveals.

Silence, like aesthetic distance, is a revealing mode of presence that opens us to the rich diversity in unity of all people, events, and things. It calms our judgmental tendency to see only the imperfections that hide the bigger picture.

Silence grants us the gift of stillness when we are dying to speak; it facilitates realistic evaluation of our situation and the serenity to live with what words fail to express. When we drain our mind of clever calculations, when we quiet our arrogant estimation of those around us, when we are simply grateful for being who we are, silence may wash over us in waves of inner peace.

Prayer: *Lord, give us the grace to see silence as the mother of prayer and not to fear the revelations of your will it discloses. In this citadel of stillness, let us think more clearly about our birth and our death. Draw us in these desert spaces to the threshold of repentance, for only in the silence of total transcendence can we find the courage to continue our task on earth and to do so with integrity.*

5 Release through Repentance

> To repent is one of the hardest things in the world,
> yet it is basic to all spiritual progress.
> It calls for a complete breakdown
> of our prideful self-assurance,
> a stripping away of the cloak of prestige
> that is woven from our petty successes,
> a breaking of the innermost citadel of our self-will.
>
> —*Catherine de Hueck Doherty*

Hearts neither ready nor willing to change resist the call to repentance. The reasons are not difficult to ascertain. Every old habit of self-centeredness by which we once lived has to be relinquished. No sooner do we let go of our ego than its tentacles threaten to reroot themselves like tenacious vines. No matter how many times we tear them out or think we have dug them up, they reappear.

Pride is like a magician with a million tricks up his sleeve. We pretend to be humble but proceed to manipulate everyone we meet. We exercise under the cover of a polite demeanor a secret penchant to be in control. We twist others' words to make them look bad and us much better. We list our virtues whenever we have a chance to do so. We act like clever politicians who drop names to advance their campaign.

A word like "stripping" is not easy to hear because we have grown accustomed to hiding behind a veneer of power and prestige. We've worked hard to earn a few accolades and we want others to know it. In the same breath as we announce a new appointment, we make sure everyone gasps a little when we disclose in confidence how much our salary will be. Genuine successes in the realm of the spiritual life mostly go unnoticed. They offer us little chance to chalk up a list of personal accomplishments. We think of what we do for others as nothing much at all. We feel embarrassed when they compliment us because we have already given credit where it belongs — to the Lord.

To breach the walls of "the innermost citadel of our self-will" cannot be done by the force of our own will power. It can only happen when we humble ourselves and ask for God's help. The wall of sin we must try to scale is so well fortified it can only be broken down stone by stone. The "complete breakdown of our prideful self-assurance" has to become not an occasional event but a disposition renewed day by day.

Prayer: *Lord, give us the presence of mind to listen to your gentle invitations as well as to your firm commands. Remind us that when we turned away from you, you returned to us to forgive our failings. Lift us over hurdles of willfulness we thought we could scale on our own. Remove from us the illusion that we are anything but sinful souls in need of redemption. Strip away every semblance of our pride-form so that the deepest Christ-form of our being can come to the fore. Break through the barriers erected by our self-will and, by means of your grace, liberate us from these prisons of our own making.*

6 Christ at the Center

> To become converted, you must fight your way
> past the deceitful voice within.
>
> —*Augustine of Hippo*

Though some highly blessed and chosen souls may experience a sudden, dramatic about-face on the road to life's transformation, Augustine's tale convinces us that instant *metanoia* is usually not the way God chooses for us. He reminds us on every page of his *Confessions* that it takes a long time to become converted. One obstacle after another has to be peeled away like the thick skin that covers the sweet pulp inside a papaya.

We must literally fight our way past the almost impenetrable fortifications erected by our own ego. The illusion by which we live is that, weak as we are, we are really all-powerful. One lie piles up on top of the other until the deceitful castle we have built begins to crack like frozen candle wax. Lights we thought we could trust become dark shadows of sin on our soul. Augustine's were legion: vainglory, fornication, and disobedience had become such habitual faults that he had no choice but to don the armor of a new knight of faith whose weapons would be humility, chastity, and obedience.

Each of us has to spend time sorting out the true from the false voices that impinge upon our soul.

Like good servants we must clean our inner house before it is too late. We may then find that what is true brings us home to the calm harbor of peace and joy whereas what is false throws us like broken shells into the stormy sea of discontent and unhappiness. Augustine's conversion brought him to the point of attending solely to God's voice within his heart. All other voices fell silent the moment Christ became the center of his life.

Conversion of heart occurs each time we replace selfish sensuality by the selfless act of laying down our lives for others (cf. Jn 15:13). What we give up in egoism we gain in intimacy with the Trinity. Inner tension decreases. Relaxed presence to the Lord increases. We see with eyes of faith that we are here to transform the world into the house of God. What exhausts us is not the dedicated performance of duty but the tense, willful way in which we go about it. Now is the time to rest in the Lord and let him guide our destiny.

Prayer: *Lord, shut our ears to the seductive voices cajoling us in deceitful whispers to choose self over you. Open our ears to your truth resonating in the inmost chambers of our heart. Let us, like Augustine, put on the Lord, Jesus Christ. May you be our Victor over every lying voice we hear from within or without. Grant us the gifts of continual conversion and ceaseless prayer to fortify our heart for the journey of faith that ends and begins when we see you face-to-face.*

7 God Known and Unknown

> God's essence, indeed, is incomprehensible utterly transcending all human thought; but on each of God's works his glory is engraved in characters so bright, so distinct, and so illustrious, that none, however dull and illiterate, can plead ignorance as their excuse.
>
> —*John Calvin*

The incomprehensibility of the Godhead transcends any name we might attach to the mystery, any thoughts we might formulate about it. In this realm, we enter the *via negativa* or the way of negation. It means that no sooner do we find a word by which to express the nature of God than we must negate it as inadequate. This *apophatic* inclination keeps us humble. We laugh at our feeble attempts to master the mystery and behold in awe and wonder all that we will never know. We temper the *hubris* that pretends to define everything. We bow to the mystery that transcends "all human thought."

Complementing the *via negativa* is the *via positiva* or the *via affirmativa* by which we celebrate the glorious array of God's works in the universe. We see his epiphany engraved on earth, fire, air, and water, on all the elements of creation and, most of all, in the incarnation of his Son. We behold the character of Christ etched on our hearts through the grace of baptism. This *cataphatic* immanence of God complements our wordless reverence for God's *apophatic* transcendence.

Calvin rightly claims that a person would have to be blind, deaf, and dumb to miss these manifestations of the mystery, revealed so brightly, so distinctly, at every waking moment. Are we so dulled by a stressful existence that we never take time to praise God's presence in the rising and setting of the sun, in a meal we enjoy or a musical symphony that takes our mind off our troubles? Are we so oblivious to the attributes of God that we cannot read them in the text of daily life?

To cultivate openness to the essence of God in everydayness, we must come to the same conclusion Calvin reached: that "on each of God's works his glory is engraved." God's works may hide themselves amidst a kaleidoscope of differences, but if we look beyond the surface of a person's appearance, we may see the miracle of his or her likeness to God.

Prayer: *Lord, in our quest for knowledge of universe and humanity, let us remember who we are: godlike creatures, not gods. Help us to be faithful servants and loyal friends chosen by you to tend your works and to see in them evidence of your glory. Cure us of spiritual illiteracy. Replace our penchant for forgetfulness by appreciation of your transcendence, by awe for your hidden messages and their sudden disclosures.*

three

Give Thanks in All Circumstances

Singing in Silence

> The slightest stirring of [the] heart
> is like a voice which sings in silence
> and in secret to the Invisible.
>
> —*Isaac the Syrian*

It seems ridiculous in a noise-polluted world to lend an ear to these whispers of the heart, yet this ancient master reminds us to pay attention to its "slightest stirring." To Isaac the heart is the core of who we are. If we do not listen to our heart, we can neither discern our deepest call nor decide what we ought to do.

A paradox immediately presents itself: the "sound" of a singing heart is "silence." The messages it has for us are proclaimed "in secret." Our mind relies on visibility: Show me! Prove it to me! Our heart leans in the opposite direction; it is comfortable with the "Invisible." The subtle communications of the heart cannot be reduced to whimsical emotions, floods of high or low feelings, sudden surges of affection that flare up momentarily and as quickly fade away.

Innermost stirrings are not like that. They have remarkable staying power. When we pay attention to such whispers, their meaning unravels layer by layer. To understand what we hear may take a lifetime.

The heart operates on a timetable not reducible to any chronological category. It teaches us invisibly but substantially. To receive its song we have to be still. The pulsating rap of reason has to give way to the nearly inaudible whispers of wisdom. We must enter, as it were, the secret garden of redeeming grace where the impossible becomes possible, the complex simple, the chaotic creative. Here we walk hand-in-hand with God in an intimacy beyond knowing that can nonetheless be comprehended in silence.

These stirrings often happen when we least expect it. In the middle of a conversation or during lonely midnight hours, we may find ourselves in the presence of the mystery. We ask no questions nor do we rush to respond.

We are free to ignore these mysterious movements or to dismiss them as figments of our imagination. We can even interpret them to suit our own scripts of what God's will for us ought to be, but, to enjoy their efficacy, we need to stay as still as possible. In hushed wonder we know God is near. Love surrounds us with soft light. Words cease. Our heart beats quietly in symphonic unison with God's composition.

Prayer: *Lord, mitigate the noise in our heads so we can hear the murmuring streams of your wisdom flowing through our hearts. Yours is the voice that sings in silence, the music heard without sound. The text of your truth is recorded in invisible ink; it glows in the dark of our mind's unbelief. Teach us secrets only faith can grasp. Scale with us mountain ranges of revelation inaccessible to doubting minds. Grant us the grace to believe though we do not see.*

2. Be on Guard

> If you have never had to endure these evil tongues,
> then it is likely you have never really tried to advance
> in your faith.
>
> —Augustine of Hippo

The prowling demon of envy must never be taken lightly. A brilliant defender of the faith like Augustine had to have been the victim of lying tongues, malicious rumors, and unjust persecution, not unlike the destructive forces hurled at Christ himself, who warned us: "If they persecuted me, they will persecute you; if they kept my word, they will keep yours also" (Jn 15:20).

If all is smooth sailing we had better be on guard. Perhaps our will, not his, is being done! Our never having to endure evil tongues might mean that we are posing as faithful people, playing to the crowd's popular tunes, compromising our beliefs. In the face of such opposition, we must still live in fidelity to our calling in Christ while learning how difficult it is not to render "an eye for an eye and a tooth for a tooth" (Mt 5:38).

The history of the church reveals countless tales patterned on the same theme: faithful messengers commit themselves to Christ and accept his commission. They do all in their power, under the impetus of grace, to advance in their faith. At the same time they become targets of persecution. Experience proves the truth emphasized by the Apostle James that it is easier to tame a wild beast than the tongue, which is a cauldron of "restless evil, full of deadly poison." What other organ can demean all that is holy and "curse those who are made in the likeness of God" (Jas 3:5–9)?

If we have never been the recipient of the tongue's lashing, is it because we have compromised our beliefs and done everything in our power to place the fear of what others may think of us above our faith? Has our own tongue become a poisonous instrument, casting suspicion on the efforts others make to do their best, perhaps in ways we fail to understand? Only when we have resolved these questions can we conclude with John the Evangelist that God's fidelity to us need never be doubted and that perfect love does cast out fear (cf. 1 Jn 4:10).

In trying to follow the dictates of a Gospel-directed life, it ought not to surprise us that being in this world will arouse misunderstanding, if not outright persecution. If the prophets that preceded us had to pay the price wrought by evil tongues, why should we expect to be treated differently?

Prayer: *Lord, you promised us peace, but not without persecution. Your cross evidences the extent to which lying tongues will go to destroy all that is good. The build-up of hate may be slow, but its effects are devastating. When we know that we are under attack, give us the wisdom to withdraw in humility to the safety of your Sacred Heart. Seeking your protection in this firestorm of misdirection is our only hope. Keep us forever in your graces regardless of what worldly losses we may have to endure.*

3 Receiving Christ in Our Soul

> The Church is nothing but a section of humanity
> in which Christ has really taken form.
>
> —Dietrich Bonhoeffer

The key word in Dietrich's one-sentence summary of ecclesiology is "really." Receiving Christ into our soul is the most real event we could possibly experience. It changes us completely. It makes us happy to pay the cost of discipleship.

Dietrich saw the Church, to which we attribute institutional order, abundant resources, and worldwide prestige, as "nothing but" a wholly human tent under whose canopy dwells the Son of God, the child born in Bethlehem, the Second Person of the Blessed Trinity. It is under this weather-scarred roof, bent under the weight of the ages, historically nearly decimated by every kind of corruption, from monetary greed to sexual deviations, that the Word made Flesh chose to take form and to bless us with abundant mercy. Amidst these many betrayals, Christ offers us the golden rings of reconciliation and covenant love.

Bonhoeffer's heinous martyrdom witnesses to the fact that the Gospel, not the ideology of the Nazi party, formed his heart. His legacy would not be death and destruction but life and liberty, a legacy more resplendent and lasting than the entire Nazi war machine.

Where the passion for raw power threatened to override the upholding of human dignity, he joined the Church in honoring the downtrodden and forgotten. Where the urge to possess others' lands and goods drove away every trace of justice, he and his friends helped citizens in danger of deportation and condemnation to find avenues to freedom. By the time he received his death sentence, death itself had lost its sting. In the nakedness of his passing from this world, Dietrich taught us to have faith in the promise of life everlasting.

Prayer: *Lord, no matter how many times we betray your trust, never depart from us. The death of your faithful ones convinces us that no trial is too difficult to bear. When doubters look to us for guidance, let them see in our eyes the reflection of your radiance in our soul. Inspire them to proceed with grace by virtue of the peace, patience, and poverty of spirit you have planted there.*

4. Caring for One Another

> Without care for each other, we forget who we truly are — children of God and each other's brothers and sisters — and so cannot become parents of generations to come.
>
> —Henri J. M. Nouwen

When we care for one another as the children of God, we sense the intensity of our interconnectedness. We enjoy a relationship of spiritual generativity that enables us, whatever our state of life, to become the "parents of generations to come."

To care means to carry the cross of suffering in compassion for our own and others' vulnerability. To care means not to show mercy sporadically but to place ourselves where love needs us to be and to give to others the gifts we have received. To care means to accept our limits and to guard against pushing beyond them.

Christ, the chief caregiver, shows us how to put our gifts to the best possible use. When caring drained his energy, he paused to replace it in prayer (cf. Mk 6:30). We risk depletion of our sense of service if we allow our "savior complex" to get the best of us. Abnormal stress decreases the flow of care that identifies us, to quote Saint Teresa of Calcutta, as "tiny pens in a mighty hand."

Care, in Nouwen's view, is a lasting disposition of the heart. Outreach efforts to feed the hungry and shelter the homeless, especially after a natural disaster, edify everyone, but care is not only an emergency measure; it is a perennial outflow of love from one person or group to another, meeting all levels of need and never indifferent to the plight of the poor.

Suffering in any form evokes the giving as well as the receiving of other-centered love through repeated acts of compassion as well as during joyful moments of joint celebration. When we are at home with ourselves and others, we become more aware of the communal bonds that bind us together. Any infringement on our mutual integrity is out of the question. When we pursue courses of action faithful to Christ's call, we become most truly who we are.

Prayer: *Lord, when teachings to the contrary fill the air, let us remember the truth that we are bound together in a brotherhood and sisterhood of compassion and care. Love beyond all telling flows from your wounded hands to heal the sins of the world. Grant us the grace never to clench our fists in indifference to the plight of people abandoned in body and soul. Let no moment pass when we do not hear the cry of those in need of care in nearby neighborhoods and far distant worlds.*

5 Willing Each Other to Be

> To love someone is not first of all to do things for them,
> but to reveal to them their beauty and value,
> to say to them through our attitude: "You are beautiful.
> You are important, I trust you. You can trust yourself."
>
> —Jean Vanier

Once a poor person begged a pastor to spare her a moment. Instead he took some money out of his pocket and offered it to her. She returned it saying: "I asked to see you, not to be unseen by you."

Have we not sometimes done the same? It is easier to offer a few cents to someone in need and then dismiss them than it is to let them feel by a kind word that we find them of infinite worth to us and God.

This approach precedes our jumping to conclusions about who they are or what they need. The persons to whom we attend have to receive confirmation of their innate dignity. Many ailments may strip one of outer comeliness but never of his or her consonance with the mystery. An ugly duckling has a hidden beauty a discerning eye never misses. By contrast, suspicion and distrust incline us to conclude, that unemployed or homeless people are lazy, that they only want to take advantage of us, that the last thing we ought to do is help them. Why don't we stop to investigate the truth or falsehood of this conclusion?

By opting to stand on the common ground of our humanness, we avoid either proselyting or engaging in the kind of philanthropism that only gives under the guarantee that one receives a similar gift in return. Ulterior motives like feeling good about what we did demean both givers and receivers. The basis for any relationship cannot be what we get out of it but what we learn from it concerning our value as human beings made in the image and likeness of God. A humble, faithful heart has to be purified of any motive than to will others to be the beautiful persons God made them.

Prayer: *Lord, redirect our way of loving from that of impersonal giving to person-to-person sharing. Let it be a distinctive mark of our destiny to be givers and receivers of care. You showed us the art and discipline of meeting others where they are. You never hesitated to relieve their physical and spiritual needs. When it feels as if we are wholly spent, be there to uplift our spirit and to save us from selfishness. Temper in us the dismissive tendency to do something and be done with it as soon as possible. Let us find the grace to look beneath surface appearances to the person of beauty you have sent us to serve. Let us see your face in the poorest of the poor so that we can behold the true worth of the wounded. In the smile that lights up our face, let us mirror your own appreciative attitude towards everyone who comes our way.*

6 Freedom of Soul

> I was not born to be free,
> I was born to adore and to obey.
>
> —C. S. Lewis

The slogan, "born to be free," may justify our refusal to listen to anyone who tries to give us advice. We are *free* to use addictive substances if they give us pleasure; we are *free* to control our own body whether this means aborting a child or euthanizing an elder. Freedom without a sense of responsibility alienates us from respect for the dignity of life. We do not think twice about cheating our employer or damaging another's reputation to get a promotion we really do not deserve. We grow hard of heart, parceling out droplets of love like a rare perfume too expensive to waste on a hug of affection or a smile of encouragement.

Misunderstood freedom combined with rampant individualism is a deadly combination; it destroys the bridge of love that ought to span the distance between us and others and all that makes life more humane. We may feel "free," but the price we pay for being above it all is a terrible loneliness no frivolous distraction can alleviate.

C. S. Lewis realized that such a mockery of freedom was not God's way for him. He chose two excellent reasons for being born again. The first concerns the disposition of adoration, which places God, not the self, at the center of our life. We adore that which is higher and mightier than we are. Lewis lost all traces of *hubris* when he surrendered to Christ. He used his freedom to direct him to a bonding that guaranteed liberation at a new level and assured him that he would never be alone.

The second reason for becoming a new believer was for him to obey. Unlike unlicensed freedom, obedience teaches us to listen to our strengths and our weaknesses. Following a lengthy correspondence with the love of his life, Lewis left his isolation and became a supportive husband and friend. He listened to new disclosures of his call to become a Christian writer, who would lead many readers to the Lord. Adoration and obedience became the keys to a fulfilling life dedicated not to his own advancement but to the literary education and spiritual formation of all who crossed his path.

Prayer: *Lord, thank you for revealing to us the paradox that the only true freedom we can hope to find resides in surrender to you. Thank you for creating us with the gift of free will. Adoration, not self-adulation, is the key to fulfilling our calling. Obedience is never a burden; it is disobedience that weighs us down. Teach us to become listeners on all levels of our being. Let our heart become an open book on which you write the directions we need to seek new depths of identification with your "yes" to the Father in life and death.*

7 To Lose Is to Gain

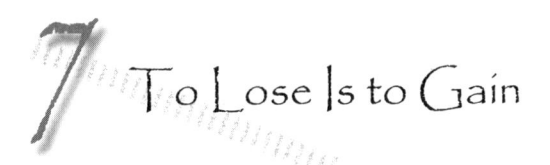

> We have all known the long loneliness,
> and we have learned that the only solution is love
> and that love comes with community.
> —*Dorothy Day*

What we know of loneliness as a devastating reality may be seen in hospital wards where patients receive few if any visitors; in half empty funeral parlors where the departed seem not to have had many friends; in loveless encounters devoid of meaning; in a mobile society where neighbors never make one another's acquaintance and where family relationships suffer because everyone scatters like dust on a deserted country road.

Dorothy Day learned that the real cure for this disease could not be found by filling the void it caused with superficial relationships, or by engaging in busy work without a center like that provided by her Catholic Worker movement. She insisted that we must pursue the opposite path: to bind ourselves heart and soul to other people, to seek their help and to be sought by them. The hardships of life may at times make us feel as if we are alone, but the truth is we are not. Christ is always with us. If we open ourselves to the people around us, we will come to know his and their love.

In the course of prayer and participation in charitable works, we may experience a movement from a-loneness to all-oneness with every human being on the face of the earth. We realize that we are *one* by virtue of the fact that we stand *alone* before God. Compassion for our failings and forgiveness of our sins create a bonding no trauma can shatter, no disappointment obscure. The Lord who calls us forth from the lonely chambers of our losses reminds us that his love is the creative force behind both solitude and community. Such togetherness in Christ means, in the words of Jean Varnier, to accept "people just as they are, with all their limits and inner pain, but also with their capacity to grow; to see the beauty inside all the pain."

It is this beauty that draws forth love out of loneliness. The thousand "what if's" that weakened our heart's capacity to risk meaningful relationships go by the wayside. The beauty inside the pain pulls us beyond our self-imposed blindness to the plight of the poor. We accept that God's surprises are always better than our plans.

Prayer: *Lord, break through the walls of loneliness behind which we are prone to hide to cover our hurt. Don't let us be afraid to be vulnerable, to admit how much we need one another. Lead us to experiences of community that are healing and freeing, never damaging or coerced. It is not our place to initiate this grace of commonality but to respond to your revelation: "Beloved, let us love one another, because love is from God; everyone who loves is born of God and knows God ... for God is love"* (1 Jn 4:7–8).

Do Not Quench the Spirit

four

Listening to Our Heart

*I prefer to speak ungrammatically and be understood
by people, rather than appear learned
and not be understood.*

—*Augustine of Hippo*

Educated in the rhetorical arts, used to philosophical debates, and living, at least before his conversion, mostly in his head, Augustine was not accustomed to listening to his heart. This plea to place understanding before the posture of appearing learned reveals the depth of Augustine's turn from a disbeliever to a defender of the faith.

Surrounded by academicians accustomed to putting a deceptive spin on the truth, Augustine may have lost his way for good had it not been for the prayers of his mother, Saint Monica, and his encounter with Saint Ambrose, Bishop of Milan, in whom he beheld the exemplary preacher and teacher he wanted to be. Behind the saint's words was a depth of learning, but from the pulpit he spoke a language everyone readily understood. His words planted in what used to be the impenetrable soil of Augustine's heart a seed of longing for God he could not suppress. This saying is a tribute to his post-conversion growth in humility. Lacking this virtue, our "apparent form" (the way we appear or want to appear to others) becomes cut off from our "core form" (what our heart tells us we ought to do to serve God and neighbor).

To follow Christ is to move from a state of routine religiosity to the practice of heroic virtue. He invites us to empty ourselves of whatever prevents our being transformed through the power of obedient love. We used to be so enmeshed in the business of the day, with all of its counter-Christian intensity, that we missed the disclosures of grace. We fooled ourselves into thinking that we could keep a part of our life under our own control when Christ asked that all of our being and doing be dedicated to him.

This integration of our inner self and our outer appearance binds our private to our public life and builds the character armor that preserves us from hypocrisy. Leaders in political and ecclesiastical positions, in centers of learning and family circles, must vow, as did Augustine, to speak from the heart with courage and compassion, without a hint of falsehood since only then can they hope to be understood.

Prayer: *Lord, listening to you preach and teach shows us what it means to be true to our word without slipping into sly deceptions for the sake of swaying others. Witnessing to our faith requires listening from within. Help us to say what we mean and mean what we say. Guard our hearts from the urgency to appear in whatever way necessary to please people and win popularity at the price of forfeiting our integrity. Intelligent as we may be, keep us simple in spirit and pure of heart. Let us find in you rest for our restless souls and reasons to recommit ourselves to being "ambassadors for Christ"* (2 Cor 5:20).

2. Mending Our Ways

> This is a warning. If you wish to fly to God,
> there are those who want to pluck your wings!
>
> —*Augustine of Hippo*

Picture yourself sitting in a waiting room clutching in your hand a ticket for the next train you believe will transport you to heaven. The first person to confront you is Mister Doubtful. "Are you out of your mind to think that someone with a history as sordid as yours will ever get past the conductor? You had better tear up your ticket while there is still time to leave the station and make amends for your mistakes. You should feel anxious and fraught with worry. It's presumptuous to be so confident of your salvation. How do you know you're worthy of redemption? There's no hope of your boarding that train and don't you forget it!"

You change your seat as fast as you can, longing for a little peace, when Mistress Envy slides in beside you. "You really consider yourself a special person, don't you? You want to be different, but you're just like everyone else. You're a fallen human being, not an angel with golden wings. Dreaming about a better life is your problem. You need to stop clinging to the sails of your high ideals and come down to earth with the rest of us. All that talk about going to the dwelling place the Divine has prepared for you is nonsense. None of us were meant to fly so stop acting as if you're the exception."

You move again, praying not to be bothered, when a finely dressed person approaches you and introduces himself as Professor Serious. "I don't doubt your dreams nor do I hesitate to laud your acumen. It's your childlike joy that gets you into trouble. You smile too much. For a person of your intelligence, you need to control the urge to laugh at your own foibles and strive instead to do something about them. The place you seek to reach calls for meticulous preparation. You can't just go there. Who will be at your destination to meet you? What if they are late? Do you have a booking to stay overnight or longer as the case may be? I notice in you a distinct lack of control. That's a nasty habit. You must not leave anything to chance. For every question there has to be a sensible answer. And, for God's sake, stop smiling when I speak to you!"

Anyone who wishes to fly heavenward, says Augustine, is likely to be deluged with objections from doubters and nay-sayers. These and many more condescending types will want to "pluck your wings," but don't let them do so. You've chosen the only worthwhile destination. Divine Mercy will escort you with lightning speed to heaven's door.

Prayer: *Lord, send into our hesitant hearts beams of blessed assurance to warm us body and soul. Keep at bay whoever wants to pluck our wings or discourage us from soaring toward heaven's door. Lift us into that longed for place of grace where doubt, envy, and worldly acclaim fall by the wayside and we throw ourselves headlong into the certitude of your tender embrace.*

3 Love Flowing Between Us

> Christ is the sun of the earth,
> and in everyone's night
> someone or something
> is needed to reflect his light,
> someone who has already absorbed it.
>
> —*Carlo Carretto*

Carretto's words remind us of anyone who has absorbed the light of Christ to such a degree that they leave us with an indelible impression of living faith. We may have known them over a lifetime of friendship or only for a moment. When others ask who has had the greatest influence on our lives, their dear faces loom before us. When they pass away the light of the world dims a little. They are our mentors and spiritual masters. In them we feel Christ's love flowing between us.

For Carretto the *Son* of man is also the *sun* of the earth. He is the axis of our existence, the center of the world. How could any of us survive its scourging without the assurance of salvation? Instead of becoming embittered by life's limits, we submit them to prayer and ask God for the grace we need to make a fresh start. Our fears of the unknown diminish. Our longing to suffer with joy becomes a reality.

There had to be some person or some book in the nights of Carretto's life which was there when he most needed encouragement. His ministry in the Sahara Desert made harsh demands upon him. Anyone in time or remembered in eternity who radiated Christ's presence would have been welcomed by him. The older and frailer we become, the more we rely on dispensers of divine light to brighten our world. Our journey deepens in a special way when we ourselves become for others Christ personified. Caretto's faithful life, his imitation of Christ, are what we remember. In him we glimpse the meaning of pure faith. We pray that by the grace of God, we, too, will be counted among those who have so absorbed the sun of Christ that others will behold in us the way through their own dark nights.

Prayer: *Lord, we have no choice but to rely on you to illumine the caverns of rebellion into which we may fall, shaking with fear and wondering who will rescue us. Suddenly you throw us a lifeline in the presence of a person who reminds us that we never walk alone. We are drawn to him or her like budding flowers to the sun, like moths to a glowing lamp. No shadows can hide the reflection of souls who have absorbed your light and refract it to everyone they meet. May we be recipients of this holy sun, forever shining in our hearts, until we soar beyond the clouds of this earth to the endless light of eternal life.*

4 From Trials to Triumphs

> If there were no trial, there would be no crown.
> If there were no wrestlings, there would be no prize;
> if no lists marked out, no honors; if no tribulation,
> no rest; if no winter, no summer.
>
> —John Chrysostom

Behind these pithy sayings is another rendition of the Paschal Mystery that pushes us past life's last boundary to the threshold of eternity. It has been said that when we come before the throne of the Most High, we will be recognized as the persons we are by the wounds we bear. For every scar on our body, tear in our eye, and hole in our heart, we will feel the commingling of sorrow for sin and joy in the face of God's unmitigated mercy. However many times we have been cut up and stitched back together during our faith journey, these wrestlings have not killed our spirit. The real prize has been won: not a wreath that loses its luster, nor wealth that disappears, but the reward of running "with perseverance the race that is set before us ..." (Heb 12:1).

Saint John Chrysostom suggests that the smallest sign of our conformity to God's will merits honors the world cannot give. Every passing hour has troubles enough of its own. We do not have to search for extra tribulations. Soon they surround us like swarms of insects, but without our having to endure their stings, we would not know the joy of a day without them.

Life itself is best understood as a series of contrasts: birth and death, suffering and salvation, cold hands and warm hearts, aridity and rain. We do not learn anything from a flat-line, homogenized existence. The Lord operates by modes of appeal, not modes of coercion. We are free to accept or reject his teachings. When we allow him to live in our heart, we become like a fertile field in which he can sow the seed of his word. Wherever he leads us, he does not leave us alone. Once we offer him our full assent, we never have to fear our limits. For him they become gifts that make our contribution to his kingdom unique.

Once in a while we need to enter into the arena of paradoxical reality where darkness becomes light; where sadness makes us doubly appreciative of a sudden burst of laughter; and where loss of life reminds us of the precious gift of a person's love.

Prayer: *Lord, you are the great exemplar of the mystery contained in these experiences of trial and triumph, of wrestling and blessed relief, of dying and rising. Grant that our seeking of any accolade will not be an end in itself but a sign that we are trying to live in conformity to your will. Around every bend of the road of life, new burdens weigh us down. Help us to see and accept that without facing these tribulations, we might never come to rest. When the winter of the heart descends upon us, let it be but a stage along the way to a springtime of hope.*

5 Unflinching Faith

> ...There are long periods in the lives of all of us, and of
> the saints, when the truth revealed by faith
> is hideous, emotionally disturbing, downright repulsive.
>
> —*Flannery O'Connor*

An observation as honest as this bursts those illusory bubbles about what it means to believe. It would be untrue to say that an ounce of faith dispels a pound of dark nights or that congratulatory notes are the order of the day for those who suffer some form of martyrdom for what they believe. The life of our Lord, like the lives of the saints, paints the opposite picture. The executioners who released wild beasts into the arena to devour the first Christian martyrs found their singing for joy to be "downright repulsive."

Belief is not a buffer zone for every ill wind that blows our way. If we accept Jesus Christ as our savior, we must be ready to go beyond the sweet sensation of saying "I believe" and be willing to choose the narrow way, take up our cross and follow him (cf. Lk 13:24). None of us knows the day or the hour when God may ask us to do something that seems at first glance beyond our capacity. Why the mystery operates in this way is not easy to understand. History shows that God chooses not the strong but the weak, not the powerful but the powerless, not learned teachers but poor tax collectors, all of whom accomplished tasks that exceeded their strength.

Humanly speaking, what God asks of us — to believe even though we do not see — seems utterly impossible. Yet, spiritually speaking, new life comes forth the moment we make this leap of faith into the unknown. The time required to test the truth revealed to us may be short or long, but the pledge of obedience is a risky business under any circumstance. So disturbing was Christ's experience in the garden of Gethsemane that he sweat blood (cf. Lk 22:44). Will any less be asked of us?

Prayer: *Lord, in all honesty we must admit that professing our faith is one matter, living it another. When the time of testing is upon us, there is no guarantee that we will not run the other way. Our patience in pain may grow thin. Keep us always in your sight, especially when others consider nonsensical our conviction that providence will provide. Send your Spirit to guide us, lest we choose the route of routinized religion in place of heroic virtue. Help us to resist the temptation to adapt our ways of witness to the ways of the world, however outrageously disturbing and "downright repulsive" they may prove to be.*

6 Following the Spirit's Leading

> The most desirable prayer is that where we can quite pour out our soul and freely talk with God.
>
> —John Wesley

From the lips of this renown Christian preacher, we receive the assurance that prayer is above all an honest exchange between us and God. When we pray, we must have no doubt that God listens and responds as much to our praises, petitions, intercessions, and thanksgivings as to our doubts, angers, fears, and conflicts. Whether being still or baring our soul, we are free to talk with our Beloved. Deeper experiences of union and communion occur when we pay attention both to the downward flow of divine inspirations and to the upward surge of human aspirations.

This understanding of prayer as a relationship with God is not without risks. The closer we come to the furnace of crucified love, the more aware we are of our sinfulness and our need for redemption. Prayer causes us to pay attention to the movements of our heart — from compunction to compassion, from fear to trust, from the inclination to tell God what to do to the courage to keep faith in the face of the unknown. What blocks our ability to listen to the insights God grants is not a lack of grace but an unwillingness on our part to wait for a reply.

Wesley's emphasis on prayer as talking freely with God reminds us that there is no reason to hide our feelings nor to be paralyzed by shame when we fail to confess them fully. Our dialogue is honest and true when we bring before God all that we think, feel, decide, and do.

The more habitual this state of union becomes, the more transforming it is. In a world that demands to see the cause behind every effect, we must be willing to live in the often incomprehensible atmosphere of sheer trust. Talking with God is not an escape from reality but a way to face whatever challenges lie before us.

This unbreakable bond of companionship with God allows us to face the harshest episodes on our journey without becoming discouraged. Prayer is to our spiritual life what breath is to our body. If we do not breathe we die physically; if we do not discourse with God, we die spiritually.

Prayer: *Lord, no day is so good that prayer ceases to be needed nor is any day so bad that prayer does not give us the strength to bear it. Our prayer time is anytime we have something to say to you, whether in the silence of pure worship or in praise of your name. By your cross and resurrection, you give us the example we need to make sense of our sufferings. Your love is better than life itself. Come, then, into the room reserved for you in our heart. Dwell there that we may talk to you whenever the Spirit moves us. Let our prayers be like reservoirs of divine energy, continually being refilled by the awareness of your presence. Reunite in splendid union recollection and participation, contemplation and action, until that day when our soul flies home free, carried by your hand through time to eternity.*

7 True Worship

> To worship is to quicken the conscience by the holiness
> of God, to feed the mind with the truth of God,
> to purge the imagination by the beauty of God,
> to open the heart to the love of God,
> to devote the will to the purpose of God.
>
> —William Temple

Sitting in any pew on an average Sunday may or may not lend itself to an experience of worship as intense as this shepherd of souls describes. A minister once said to his congregation that if the people coming into the sanctuary to pray are the same people leaving it, then his mission has failed. Either they go forth transformed in Christ or they content themselves with routine substitutes for awe, reverence, worship, and adoration.

In this posture of attentive abiding, we go before God to be fed spiritually by the truth only Divine Revelation can offer searching minds and hearts. What we take into ourselves at this depth has to be ruminated upon, digested inwardly, and assimilated into all facets of our existence. The word that is the basis of our worship may then be carried over into everyday life.

We realize how dissipated our existence has become when we attempt to quiet ourselves inwardly. How difficult it is to pay attention to what we hear! Our imagination darts like spent embers on a dying fire here, there, and everywhere. Our mind is like a corral filled with untamed horses. True worship, according to Temple, purges or purifies our imagination, directing us away from the distractions of daily life to behold the beauty of God. The architecture of the Church, the cadence of the hymns sung by the choir, the play of light through stained glass windows — all such touches of earthly beauty become pointers to the eternal splendor of the Most High.

The entire experience of worship orients us to exchanges of love beyond words. The devotion of our faith community confirms the fact that God has found a dwelling place in our hearts. Strengthened by our togetherness in this sacred space, we rededicate ourselves to a life of discipleship. We walk away from this holy ground knowing that we are better persons than we were when we went through the gate.

Prayer: *Lord, remind us through the power of your Spirit to relight the fire of our love from the moment a religious service begins to the time it ends. Awaken us from the sleep of worldly complacency to the pristine reality of what transpires around us. Teach us to worship you in spirit and in truth (cf. Jn 4:24). Let the ears of our heart vibrate with your every whisper. Transform us by the bestowal of graces so profound that your will becomes wholly our own.*

Bibliography

Augustine of Hippo. *The Confessions.* Trans. John K. Ryan. New York: Doubleday, 1960.

Bonhoeffer, Dietrich. *The Cost of Discipleship.* Trans. R. H. Fuller. New York: Touchstone, 1995.

Brother Lawrence of the Resurrection. *The Practice of the Presence of God.* Trans. Salvatore Sciuba. Washington, DC: ICS Publications, 1994.

Calvin, John. *The Institutes* in *The Protestant Reformation.* Ed. Lewis W. Spitz. Englewood Cliffs, NJ: Prentice-Hall, Inc., 1966.

Carretto, Carlo. *Letters from the Desert.* Trans. Rose Mary Hancock. Maryknoll, NY: Orbis Books, 1972.

Ciszek, Walter J. with Daniel Flaherty. *He Leadeth Me.* Garden City, NY: Image Books, Doubleday, 1975.

Chrysostom, John. *On the Incomprehensible Nature of God.* Trans. Paul W. Harkins. Washington, DC: The Catholic University of America Press, 1982.

John Climacus. *The Ladder of Divine Ascent.* Trans. Colm Luibheid and Norman Russell. Classics of Western Spirituality. New York: Paulist Press, 1988.

Coles, Robert. *Spiritual Life of Children.* Boston: Houghton Mifflin Co., 1990.

Day, Dorothy. *The Long Loneliness.* Harper: San Francisco, CA: 1997.

Doherty, Catherine de Hueck. *Poustinia: Christian Spirituality of the East for Western Man.* Notre Dame, IN: Ave Maria Press, 1975.

Flaubert, Gustav. *Madame Bovary.* New York: Penguin Books, 2002.

Isaac the Syrian. *The Wisdom of Saint Isaac the Syrian.* London: Fair Acres Publications, 1997.

John XXIII, Pope. *Journal of a Soul.* Trans. Dorothy White. New York, NY: McGraw-Hill Book Co., 1965.

Lavelle, Louis. *The Meaning of Holiness.* New York: Pantheon Books, 1954.

L'Engle, Madeleine. *The Weather of the Heart.* Wheaton, IL: Harold Shaw Publishers, 1978.

Lewis, C. S. *Surprised by Joy: The Shape of My Early Life.* New York, NY: Harcourt, 1956.

Nouwen, Henri J. M. *The Wounded Healer: Ministry in Contemporary Society.* Garden City, NY: Doubleday & Company, 1972.

O'Connor, Flannery. *Letters of Flannery O'Connor.* Ed. Sally Fitzgerald. New York. Farrar, Straus, Giroux, 1979.

Percy, Walker. *The Last Gentleman.* New York: Avon Books, 1978.

Price, Reynolds. *A Whole New Life: An Illness and a Healing.* New York: Scribner, 2003.

Richard of Saint Victor. *The Twelve Patriarchs, The Mystical Ark.* Trans. Grover A. Zinn. Classics of Western Spirituality. New York: Paulist Press, 1979.

Temple, William. *Nature, Man and God.* Whitefish, MT: Kissinger Publishing Co., 2003.

Vanier, Jean. *The Broken Body: Journey to Wholeness.* New York: Paulist Press, 1988.